Praise for Katie Kemple's
Big Man

Reading *Big Man* feels like sitting with an old friend on a comfy couch and exchanging stories about parents late into the night. These poems contain vulnerable vignettes: a child discovering a wedding photo of her dad with his first wife, a grown woman eating ice cream sandwiches from her father's freezer after his death while remembering his stories of war, and many moments in between. "My dad, a bear of a guy, had a heart / of honey: sweet and stuck," Kemple writes, and readers are so fortunate that she's chosen to share him with us.

—Katie Manning, author of *Hereverent* and *28,065 Nights*

Big Man guides us through an unflinching portrait of a father. But perhaps, more importantly, we witness a journey from father as mythic figure to father as human. Kemple's masterful remembrance is a difficult one, as the people closest to us are the most difficult to catalogue because we are close observers of too much. But Kemple does just that—honors this remembrance and the many names and ways a person is remembered, recognizing all the "small things we might have passed into his big hands."

—Su Cho, author of *The Symmetry of Fish*

These poems sing of the everyday world, the everydayness of life, love, and family, lifting us via the poet's act of attention into an almost spiritual realm. In these pages, through the eyes of his daughter, you'll fall enthralled with her father, with his "heart / of honey: sweet and stuck." Along the journey you'll fall back in love with your own life. If you have someone to hug, go hug them. If not, hug yourself.

—Christopher Citro, author of *If We Had a Lemon We'd Throw It and Call That the Sun*

Swift—& blunt w/grief: "We opened the earth's / lid and buried him there." Katie Kemple's twenty-five poem ode to her dad, *Big Man*, is personal, specific, vivid—"like a forest of green recycling arrows"—& full of love, such love, love the lucky of us briefly know & mourn.

—Adam Golaski, author of *Voice Notes*

Big Man

Chestnut Review Chapbooks, an imprint of Chestnut Review LLC
Ithaca, New York

https://chestnutreview.com
ISBN: 978-1-965158-12-8

Big Man

Katie Kemple

Chestnut Review Chapbooks

In memory of my father

Patrick W. Kemple

CONTENTS

The Wedding Album

We found our father's first wife
in the closet upstairs, behind
the child size door my sister and I
cracked open, under the naked
pull-light in a maroon leather album.
That 1970s pigment gave a warm
glow to the photos. Dad in a dark
tux, white carnation in the lapel.
The lady next to him brunette
like mom but angular, wore
glasses. At six and four, we didn't
understand. I took the album
to Mom fresh out of the shower,
penciling her face in. The sight
of it creased her eyes: "Pat!"
she hollered. Dad arrived, took it
back, ushered us to the table,
said: "You know how your kitten
died?" Hit by a car in front of our
house. He said his first wife died
in a similar accident. My sister
and I must have hugged him,
the memory of our cat stinging.
But I only remember tugging
my sister's hand to play outside.
When night fell, Dad sat alone
by the hearth stoking the flames,
the wedding album man, a stranger.
He saw me there and looked away,
back to the blazing fire he created.
I didn't know who I was anymore.

Portrait of a Father

The newspaper print shows Dad
at an easel as a boy with two girls
watching as if he were Picasso
his left arm over the canvas.
He liked working with his hands,
tinkering with gears, chopping
wood, mending shirts with thread
and needle. Can't say we inherited
a piece of art. His paid medium:
human, molding students into
hands-on professionals. Some
painted nails or cars, others entered
culinary arts. My sister and I
squint at the print to guess what
he's making, but it's blanched by
the flash. He'd barely started.

VFW Memorial Day Parade

They crowned me the poppy queen
when I was four. Mom pinned a tiara
of red remembrances, fabric flowers
with wire tails and black centers
on top of blonde pigtails.
I rode in the parade on my father's
shoulders, wearing a white dress
from Sears Roebuck with bells
sewn in the hem. Dad wore his
Vietnam Veterans hat, blue jeans,
tinted glasses. My hands on his
beard grasped the edge of a smile.
We marched from Main Street
to the VFW bar. We kids ran free
in the yard, palms dropping potato chip
alms to the outstretched arms of grass
while the bar tender pulled draft
after draft after draft for our dads.

Feminist Father

When he married mom, he didn't know
he'd joined a matriarchy. I arrived first,
then my sister. Three against one. He'd
grown up with three brothers, survived
seminary and Air Force. It didn't
qualify him to make Plaster of Paris
villages for our pastel My Little Ponies.
No one taught him to construct the used
dreamhouse he'd found for Christmas.
He'd go with us if we wanted to walk
our baby dolls in pink prams, chaperoned
Girl Scout field trips, drove us to visit
colleges. He stayed calm when we got
in trouble. He only said, *what are you,*
stupid? once. Apologized immediately.
He didn't protest when we paraded out
in barely-there-dresses. If he'd wanted
sons, he never told us. He gave us
confidence, said we could be anything.

Childhood

At the science museum, he rolled his sleeping bag
out on the floor of the physics exhibit, next to his
daughter and dozens upon dozens of Girl Scouts
from across New England. Like a field of cocoons,
an infestation, they'd tucked in squirming at first
and then near stillness among the towering glass
and metal displays. His daughter slept beside him
with her mouth open, a gentle snore. And soon,
he too fell asleep.

He dreamt they were back in the garage at home,
examining the pulley system. He showed her how
to load it with a bale of hay. But in the dream,
she flew up instead, laughing and tumbling in
the air. His arms ached from the weight of the bundle.
He couldn't let go. And he couldn't reach out to her
either. He felt a music in his chest swirl and woke
to the cartoon sounds of a machine in the exhibit.

First the plink

                                 then the roll

a

       tick

             tick

                  tick

and a

xylophone

fall

His daughter's sleeping bag empty now. He saw

her with a friend at the foot of the contraption.
They covered their mouths with laughter. Clearly
They'd pulled the lever. Woke the whole floor.
He couldn't help but think that sounded
the end. Childhood gone. Life up in the air.

Breakthrough

My best friend and I took up tennis, played
at my house hitting balls against the garage.
The pop, pop, pop a constant as Dad tinkered
on the other side of the wall. We broke
the peaked attic window. Broke the ones
on the door, too. My friend fearful we'd get
in trouble. But we never got a talking-to.
Maybe Dad knew giving permission meant
having the glass break. Maybe he sensed
what we'd be up against. I still feel it in me
(our neon green resiliency) where our screams
of joy bounced free. Dad permitted it. Let us
beat and break and win.

Peppermint Twist

Dad's favorite doo-wop song came out
when he entered middle school,
that sticky music coated his inner ears'
love canal, twisted red and white up
the swirl of his cochlea, twirled down
the stick of his body. Dad danced to this.

Round and round. Up and down.

His life in front of him like a pine tree
flush with Christmas gifts. He could
still dream of a career as a scientist.
His limbs could twist into it, knees
swiveling, legs flexible, feet free to tap
the beat, shoes shining the floor clean!

One, two, three kick, one two three jump.

Catholic kids in baby boom masses
swinging around the room. Conflict
approaching in their side-view,
that night only sweetness. Plastic
wrapped lives, unopened, crisp.

a new dance, and it goes like this...

The Punching Room

Maybe I was thirteen, out with my dad
for the day and we had to stop by
the vocational school where he worked
as a special ed teacher. I followed him
through the rooms in the uninterested
way new teenagers do. But the padded
room stopped me. Not much bigger
than a closet. What's that? I asked.
Sometimes, he said, *the kids here need*
something to punch, when a kid gets
angry enough, and we want them
to do it in a safe place. That seemed
enough of an answer to me back then.
But I'm 45 now: did I make this place up?
I picture the logistics of the system:
my dad shouldering an angry boy into
the enclosure. And how to know
when he might be safe to depart?
My dad, a bear of a guy, had a heart
of honey: sweet and stuck. He knew
how it felt to grow in a home
that stifled life. His heart pounded
his chest, bled out over decades,
burst open in isolation and let itself out.

Hitchhiker

My dad would pick up hitchhikers on the drive
to the mall, he knew them all. Past students
with hair sprayed mullets and ripped jeans,
wearing faded t-shirts of their favorite bands:
Metallica, AC/DC, Guns N' Roses, maybe.
These guys, so polite to my dad, would sit
in our car with respect, like a rubber band
in the pocket, a colorful bit of gum stuck
beneath a desk, a stray bullet that forgot
to have a target. Maybe I was mean to think
of them that way. My dad knew their names,
knew something about them, asked questions
or didn't. Most often, we sat in silence. I think
he thought he was picking himself up, my dad.

The Negotiator

They fought more frequently that summer
on the drive to the shore. As the chief
negotiator for his union Dad pushed too
far, brought management to a breaking
point. They couldn't fire him so they did
the next best thing: strip him of his post.
His punishment: a class of first graders.
Our mother, who'd taught kindergarten
for decades, did not have confidence
in his prospects. My sister and I, trapped
in the car listening, didn't dare weigh in.
I knew Dad had done the right thing.
My pride for him swelled like a king tide.
He'd negotiated a better contract.
And won! Why couldn't Mom fixate
on that? She kept knocking him, knocking
him, knocking him over. Until silence.
He rolled his window down.
Ocean air filled our lungs with a dull roar.

Table for One

On holiday weekends, or when we
had visitors, Dad would come home
with a coffee cake behind a plastic
window. Round ring of brown,
white icing dripping down the sides
like snow melting off our roof.
Walnuts on top, raisins inside.
The cake itself stale as a break room.
Something to sit on the counter
like plastic fruit as relatives and friends
maneuvered to get at better things.

Was it midnight when the reunion
occurred? Dad at peace by the glow
of the television. Documentary
about National Parks, grizzly bears.
The box balanced on his stomach,
a picnic table dressed in terry cloth.
He cut neat slices, ate each one
like an orange, licked his fingers clean.
We'd find the peel of his meal
the next day. Box undone, wings
folded into trash. Upstairs, the cake
pumped through his body
like a forest of green recycling arrows.

Red Car Poem

Never buy a red car, was my father's advice.
They get into more accidents. That's a fact, he said.
So, he purchased the plain white Plymouth
at the lot for me to drive to community college.

The truth is, I'd crashed the family car already,
accelerated down a country road embankment,
yelled: *She's gonna blow!* As me, and my sister,
and my sister's friend, and my sister's friend's dog

scrambled up the hill. I didn't even bother to turn
the engine off. A disinterested neighbor let
us in to use his phone. The paramedics strapped
me to a board and delivered me to the hospital.

My dad met me there, calm as always, with my
journal in case I wanted to capture the moment.
By then he'd already received the worst calls
a person could get in life. My accident a minor

incident. He'd lost his first wife Carol to a blood
red AMC Gremlin. A few years later, it was his
brother Eddie in a cherry red Karmann Ghia.
Soon, it was my mom's turn: hit head-on

during her morning commute. Red Buick.
She survived that one, but only after months
in a hospital. The car I'd crashed, a mere maroon,
only left my face in bruises. I dropped ten pounds

that week and squeezed into my skinny jeans,
so you know where my priorities were at.
My boyfriend came over with a vial of arnica.
I have no clue what I wrote in that journal

at the hospital. My best friend took photos
of my car, which was on display at our town's
mechanic shop (despite being unrecoverable).
The visual, a scarlet letter, proof that I

was trouble. I don't know what it says about
my father that he blamed the car. At the dealership,
he told me to get behind the wheel. I drove.
I wrote the road in our paper-white Plymouth.

Big Man

The walk from the air-conditioned truck
to the mall turned him into a popsicle,
sweat dripping down his tanned forehead.
He had a big build in the arms and shoulders,
strong like bull, he'd told his daughters.
He didn't move easy, but well enough
in his Gold's Gym t-shirt with the sleeves
cut off, his ancient mesh shorts. He had
nearly made it to the door, its chill relief,
when a voice sizzled through the air.
A six-year-old girl exploded into him:
Mr. Kemple! Mr. Kemple! Mr. Kemple!
Hollering like he was a celebrity, not her
first-grade teacher. She hugged his bad leg,
wrapped around him like a Band-Aid.
And for a moment, he could acknowledge
it, the pent-up pain, the strain, how hard it
felt to move. Maybe the girl had no one
at home to hug. They both took a break
from being tough and melted there together.

Eating disorder meet cute.

Watching James Gandolfini in a rom-com,
his big vulnerable body, strong and hurt,
his tenderness toward the female lead,
who of course has an eating disorder,
reminds me of my father. My mother.
Bookends and mirror twins of America's
number one industry and obsession: weight.
In the movie, the jumbo popcorn scene
must be tempered with a discussion
about extra butter, a shaming, a crushing
of the soft white fluffiness into a flat bug.
My childhood was filled with bags
of microwave popcorn, dampened
with Diet Coke. My distinct lower abdomen,
house to the intestines, a pantry of sorts.
My dance teacher once told me:
That's where you need to drop
the weight. For the rest of that summer,
I ran every day. My dad liked to tell us
how far he used to run, before the busted
knees, before the weight piled on.
I heard it as shame. We all knew mom
could beat him in a race, she ran every day,
a taut suntanned bone. The lesson:
Keep moving, keep moving, keep moving.
In the movie, Gandolfini gets the girl.
I blush to see them kiss, as if they were
my parents. When the credits roll, Gandolfini's
end recalls itself. Like my dad, the path
to his heart blocked up. Nowhere to run.
Those big guys too tender for this earth.
I wish they could have eaten in the open,
savored every finger-licking moment
in their wild, butyraceous bodies.

Home Gym

Dad carried the boxes up the stairs
to the laundry room, up all night
assembling the system of pullies,
screwing bars to benches,
piling the weights up the spine of it.
No excuses now! He'd drop
the weight like mom wanted.
He didn't need to prove his strength
to me. He split wood, shoveled snow,
climbed twenty-foot ladders to stain
the house. His pain soothed after
by two aspirin, a beer, hard pretzels.
He'd use the gym later, he said,
when he got his energy back.
He played hoops as a teen, he'd
tell me. Ran five miles to town!
But what I knew of his body
came after the war: busted knees,
round belly. His gym evolved without
him. The bar became a hanger
for mom's dresses. The bench
dried our woolen sweaters.
The weights grew a coat of lint.
That's how we found it decades
later, when my sister and I returned
to help him sell the house.
I offered to take the gym down,
loosened the metal bones
of his colossus, cracked the bench
into legs, carried each weight
like a baby down the stairs,
loaded the parts into his truck.
I drove us to the recycling center.

He hung back as I threw the bars,
sinuous pullies and dusty weights
into the pit. A scream without lips.

PTSD

In December, bins of mixed nuts return
to grocery stores in their hard armor,
polished helmets and bullet-proof gear
to prevent a fall from ruining their interior.
They were meant to drop like a ticket

to earth. My father, a peculiar squirrel,
leaned over his brown lacquered bowl
split down the middle, like a walnut's
membrane, separated the sides, one
for shells, one for bodies. His finger

joints strong as Brazil nuts, pressed
down on the metal cracker, until his
subject snapped in two. Meticulous.
Neat. He knew how to free every
speck of meat from its wooden cage.

His teeth ground the teardrop almonds,
brainiac walnuts, submarine shaped
pecans. Or the humble peanuts whose
shells could be rubbed off with a thumb,
while he watched the wonders of nature

on the big TV, or the horrors of war.
War documentaries meant a glass
of beer or two, a Jameson. Would mean
I would find him there at midnight,
cracked open, too soft for me to bear.

Final Flame

Mom wanted to buy another candle.
Cancer plus chemo burns at both ends.
And Dad said: *More candles, why?*

They were 70 bucks a pop
at a boutique down the street.
Mom said: *I want to buy them now.*

They're no good in a casket.
And Dad lost it. Stepped outside,
started crying. Penny pinching

couldn't fix this. His heart a wick
for Mom and she lit it. We bought
another candle. Two more, three.

We bought every scent they sold,
week by week, room by room,
burning the house bright

like a cathedral. That's how she
wanted to go, like Sand and Dune;
like Ski House; and Peony Powder Room.

Like Champagne Penthouse. Going
out in White Grapefruit Cabana.
Dying bright in Black Pomegranate.

Beached

We followed our father into
the waves where his knees
had the support of the ocean
and he could be the kind of dad
who could play, leaping high,
dunking. He taught us to dive
through walls of water, to eye
the horizon for the next wave's
motion, to pick ourselves up
when we tumbled like socks
in the roar and landed on shore
with suits of sand. His large
body buoyant, we never doubted
he'd be okay. I had my kids
with us at the beach by the time
his foundation faltered. Time,
salt, and water crack every man.
He stepped sideways back
to shore, waves pounding
his calves beneath the joints.
He crashed into the sand
and didn't get up.

No Meds Monday

is what my sister and I called it
when we couldn't get ahold of Dad.
We had a nurse come Tuesday to
Sunday to ensure he took his pills.
On Mondays he decided, or was it
he remembered, or didn't, to take
his meds or not? The metformin
for diabetes, the baby aspirin for
heart attacks, and whatever else he
had in that plastic box of windows
with the days abbreviated. Stress,
he'd tell us, killed people. Couches
and television: the best medicine!
Did you get through to Dad, I'd ask
my sister, and she'd say no. And
we'd both go: No Meds Monday!
A miracle when he remembered
to call on my thirty-eighth birthday.
The line cut out mid-sentence.
Well, the phone decides, I said,
retelling it to my sister, laughing.
We knew Dad wouldn't call back.

Candid

I made Dad a plate of sunny-side-up eggs
brought it to him on the overstuffed sofa
navigating furniture too large for a condo.
The hutch behind his shoulder contained
miniatures of his trips with mom: swizzle
sticks in Irish shot glasses, a Swiss woods-
man nutcracker, pastel Bermuda cottages.
In front of him: reruns of *Seinfeld*, election
coverage, incontinence ads. Only the glass
coffee table dared reflect his life back.
He hid it beneath newspapers. He ate off
a dish with a village painted on it. People
laughing. Festive houses. The runny yolks
provided a sunny sort of day. He ate
watching TV. I left him that way. I left
him because he liked it that way. Closed
his door slowly, peering through the crack.
An aperture: I took his final photograph.

Expiration

Ants leave their dead for two days
before the body is carried to a graveyard,
or so the experts on the Internet write,
leaving me to wonder which ants?
Fire, leafcutter, or the September ones
that enter our house in search of water?
And what of this graveyard described
as a *pile of dead bodies*? They say it
takes two days because the ants don't
know the body's dead until it releases
oleic acid. Humans have been known
to walk by dead humans, not knowing
they were dead or not caring. Humans
also came up with the insidious test:
put oleic acid on a live ant and watch
it struggle as another ant carries it
to the grave. When an ant perceives
a dead ant, it alters her day. No longer
following the scent of food, obligation
takes its place. She counter clocks
the body back to its grave. When my
father had a heart attack, he called 911.
I found that out when I answered
my phone at the grocery store, putting
chicken, apples, ice cream down
the conveyor belt. "Everything alright?"
I asked the woman from my father's
assisted living condo. "No," she replied.
I took a plane back to New York.
His body on ice, then processed, delivered
in a lap-sized box. His military headstone
came with an expiration date. I thought
of his habit of eating expired foods.

He would sniff containers, trusting
his senses first. We opened the earth's
lid and buried him there. I marched back,
returned to my regular job and tasks,
placed myself down the conveyor belt.
At the grocery store, I checked out.

Last Bite

After, I can only remember the ice cream
sandwiches left in Dad's freezer. Generic,
on sale brand, the way he liked them.
Wrapped in a sterile white sheet of paper.
Folded with military precision. A twin bed.
A box of them. Each day while clearing
out his condo, I unwrapped a new one,
chewed the soft chocolate lid and bottom,
the white creamy middle, crumpled
the sheet on his kitchen table like a teen
might have left an unmade bed. Also
on the table, photos from the war. Dad
in his uniform, before a beard covered
his face, before the glasses. Air Force jet
in the background. They gave him a job:
package the bodies as they returned
from the front. When he'd talked about
it, he cried like those men had just died.
My mind numbed staring in his freezer.
I consumed the last bit of his sweetness.

National Dad Died Day

Dad died on National Ceiling Fan Day,
Global Company Culture Day. Hug A
Greeting Card Writer Day. International
Equal Pay Day. National Cheeseburger
Day. U.S. Air Force Day. He would
have liked the last two best. If heaven
exists, they'd greet him with a double
cheeseburger. A greeting card writer
would give him a hug. He'd finally get
paid as much as Mom! A ceiling fan
would cool him off. And the buddies
he lost in the Air Force would welcome
him home. He would feel, up there,
part of a global culture. At ease until
he started to wonder which wife would
find him first? Or worse. His mother.

Heart failure as River Styx.

If my father had made it from his
condo to an ambulance to a hospital,
would he still be here? The river
of his blood filled with flotsam
and jetsam instead. I picture him
making that journey to the afterlife
on a raft down the Hudson of his
life past Kingston, Poughkeepsie,
and the Newburg-Beacon bridge,
past Westchester and back home
to Yonkers again. Playing his horn
proud and loud, playing it standing
precariously on the raft, bare chested
his freckles reflected in the Hudson
joined their brothers in the stars.

Sunday Morning Visitation

Dad lives in a donut shop now,
the parchment wings flying
down to meet the cruller I select.

He's the warmth of the cheap
coffee, its bitter tang
meant for sugar and cream.

I drink it black, back in my car,
lid off, dipping the hollow
pastry in torn chunks into

brown metallic sauce. The way
Dad had done, eating
a variety pack in his car

to avoid Mom's counting gaze,
savoring another glazed.
He wasn't happy to outlive

her. I took after him, doughy
and soft in the center,
despite Mom's molding—

never met a donut I didn't
like. But I'll visit
her next, at ballet class, kicking

the shit out of air, with Dad's
blood leaping in my veins,
the two of them duking it out,

making my pulse rush. Until,
empty cup and slippers flung
off, I fold my sugared wings.

Our Father

At the cemetery our father has two
headstones. One shared with our mother:
names and death only. The other one:
Air Force Sergeant. Four years of war.
His name carved into the stone of U.S.
imperialism. His triangular flag added
to the mosaic of servicemen. Here he
will not be the father, teacher, union
negotiator, driver of teenagers, joyful
eater of fried chicken, ice cream, pizza.
Born. Air Force. Died. He had a wife.
We leave heart shaped rocks, sea glass,
shells and pinecones. Small things we
might have passed into his big hands.

Acknowledgements

Thank you to the editors and journals where version of these poems first appeared. Your acceptances encouraged me to continue writing this collection.

"The Punching Room," *San Diego Poetry Annual 2023-2024*, Steve Kowit Prize finalist

"Eating Disorder Meet Cute," *Drunk Monkeys*

"Expiration" and "Hitchhiker," *The Ilanot Review*

"Red Car Poem," *Pembroke Magazine*

"Sunday Morning Visitation," *JMWW*

"Candid," *SWWIM*

Thank you to Maria S. Picone, and *Chestnut Review*, for seeing the potential in *Big Man* and providing such thoughtful edits and appreciations as we worked through drafts. I couldn't imagine this manuscript in better hands.

Thank you to my sister Annie, my constant companion on the journey of daughterhood, sisterhood, and life. And to my husband David and our kids Sparrow and Rosalia for their encouragement as I devoted hours each week to drafting, editing, and submitting.

Thank you to my "poetry-family" and first readers: Joe, Filiz, Carol, and Frank. Your feedback and companionship helped me hone this work.

Thank you to the Martha Vineyard Institute of Creative Writing (MVICW), whose generous parent-fellowship program allowed me to devote a week to work on this collection.

About the Author

Katie Kemple's poems are published in or forthcoming from *Beloit Poetry Journal*, *Ploughshares*, and *The South Carolina Review*. More of her work can be found at katiekemplepoetry.com. *Big Man* is her debut collection.

www.ingramcontent.com/pod-product-compliance
Lightning Source LLC
Chambersburg PA
CBHW030528130626
46549CB00007B/3146